Glynn Chris

BEST OF BREAK
COOK BO

British Broadcasting Corporation

Published by the
British Broadcasting Corporation
35 Marylebone High Street
London W1M 4AA

ISBN 0 563 20316 1
First published 1984

Typeset by Phoenix Photosetting, Chatham
Printed in England by
Mackays of Chatham Ltd

Contents

Bread and Baking

The Store Cupboard

Christmas Time

Conversion Tables

All these are approximate conversions which have either been rounded up or down. Never mix imperial and metric measures in one recipe, stick to one system or the other.

Oven temperature

Mark 1	275°F	140°C
2	300°	150°
3	325°	170°
4	350°	180°
5	375°	190°
6	400°	200°
7	425°	220°
8	450°	230°
9	475°	240°

Volume

2 fl oz	55 ml
3	75
5 (¼ pt)	150
½ pt	275
¾	425
1	570
1¾	1 litre

Measurements

⅛ inch	3 mm
¼	½ cm
½	1
¾	2
1	2.5
1¼	3
1½	4
1¾	4.5
2	5
3	7.5
4	10
5	13
6	15
7	18
8	20
9	23
10	25.5
11	28
12	30

Weights

½ oz	10 g
1	25
1½	40
2	50
2½	60
3	75
4	110
4½	125
5	150
6	175
7	200
8	225
9	250
10	275
12	350
1 lb	450
1½	700
2	900
3	1 kg 350 g

Introduction

The Gosh Factor

Well, what an experience. Now the first year of being Food Reporter and Chef for *Breakfast Time* is over, I can scarcely believe how much we have packed in. Over 150 programmes of tips, recipes and reports have taken me from the cockle beds of Swansea on a burning summer's day to New York at 4 am in temperatures of 18° below freezing. From the great London markets of Spitalfields and Billingsgate to strawberry fields in Kent, a black pudding factory in Derby, the streets of Paris and London's Chinatown. From an urban farm where I patted a Gloucester Old Spot pig to sailing in on the tide with Plymouth's fishermen, Fast Food Exhibitions, a Kosher restaurant, cheese factories and a jumbo-jet flight to look at Miami's supermarkets. My main reaction is – gosh!

I hope that your reaction is the same, for the Gosh Factor is the basis of everything I have done.

There is a well-known show-business phrase that exhorts one to 'Make 'em laugh'. But on *Breakfast Time* I simply want you to say 'Gosh'. I know few of you have the time to concentrate on complicated recipes or deeply investigative reports. Thus I feel my job is well done if just one factor sticks in your mind and makes you say – well, you've guessed it – Gosh, that sounds delicious, or Gosh, I didn't know that.

Many of the Gosh Factors you have most appreciated have been the simplest tips, such as cooking a turkey on its side, or how to make cabbage interesting. One woman almost crushed me to an early death with appreciation of my way of cooking rhubarb with no water and some grated orange peel. She swore it had changed her life and that her children now spoke to her. What a responsibility!

To collect all the simple Gosh Factors of the year would need a book hundreds of pages long. So this is a collection of the recipes most requested during the year, but which you may not have had time to jot down or forgot to write in for.

Thank you for the tremendous interest and support you have given me. As I look forward to this next year I have only one thing to say to you all – Gosh, I think you are terrific!

Glynn Christian

Starters

Chicken and Toasted Barley Broth

Serves 4–6

This good old-fashioned treat costs just pence if you use your chicken bones and vegetables to make your own stock.

1½–2 oz toasted pearl barley
2½ pints chicken stock, strained
or
2 chicken stock cubes
8 oz mixed grated root vegetables
2½ pints water

To toast the pearl barley, simply stir over medium heat in a non-stick pan. You can use a little oil if you like. Once evenly brown, remove from the heat and continue stirring until the pan has cooled . . . if the pan is very hot it may be better to tip out the grains.

If you have the time, soak the toasted grains overnight by just covering with water. This increases their sweetness.

To make the broth, put the stock, or the cubes, vegetables and water into a saucepan with the toasted barley (include the small amount of soaking water) and cook gently for about 1½ hours. For real rib-sticking flavour and savour you can add grated vegetables even if you start with well-flavoured chicken stock.

Iced Avocado Soup

Serves 4–6

Avocados are now available year round and clever shoppers can often find ripe ones sold cheaply. Test for ripeness by cradling the avocado in your palm rather than bruising it with a fingertip.

2 lb ripe, firm avocados
1 pint chicken stock
½ pint cream or milk
1 tbsp lemon or lime juice
A little garlic juice
2 tsp salt
Up to 1 dsp Worcestershire sauce
Double cream to decorate

Make a purée of the avocado flesh, ensuring you have included every bit of the vital, vivid green lining to the skins. Blend well with the chicken stock and then thin to preferred texture with milk or cream. Flavour with the fresh lemon or lime juice, garlic juice (use a crusher), salt and just enough Worcestershire sauce to give a subtle bite.

Chill thoroughly, check the flavour and make any necessary adjustments. Serve topped with a swirl or dollop of double cream.

Options: Sprinkle with very finely chopped green pepper, with finely chopped green ginger, or with sprigs of mint, but don't use any type of onion. If you have no stock, use just 1 stock cube to 1 pint of water. You might also like to try heating a little of the stock with some curry powder before incorporating it. Orange juice and grated orange peel might replace the lemon. Use skimmed milk if you have a cholesterol problem.

Carrot and Orange Soup

Serves 4–6

This recipe came from Mr and Mrs Michael Foot. Although it can be delicious served cold in summer, it is much better appreciated when made with the tastier old carrots of winter.

2 oz onion
2 oz butter
½ lb carrots
2 oranges
2 pints chicken stock
Single cream and parsley or mint to decorate

Chop the onion very finely indeed, then cook until soft in the butter. Add the finely sliced carrots together with the juice of both oranges and the finely grated rind of just one of them. Once the butter is well absorbed add the stock. If you have to use stock cubes, allow only 2 for this quantity of water or their taste will be much too assertive. Simmer covered until the carrot is well softened, then sieve.

This makes a smooth thin soup which is prettily finished with a swirl of single cream and a few flat parsley or mint leaves floated on top.

Potted Chicken Livers

Serves 8 or more

The simplest of all first courses or buffet-party dishes. Some would call it a pâté, as indeed it is, but it is also good old British potting. The high fat content means such dishes last for ages when refrigerated. And instead of following the old path of serving with toast, which is a bore to make for more than a few people at a time, serve it scooped on top of an interesting salad, dribble a decent dressing over both leaves and potted livers, and enjoy with a knife and fork.

- 12 oz fatty bacon, preferably smoked
- 8 oz onion, finely chopped
- 4 oz butter
- 2 bay leaves, dry or 3–4 fresh
- 1 tsp dried thyme
- ½ tsp dried rosemary
- 1 lb chicken livers
- 1–2 capfuls sherry or brandy
- Red peppers and bay leaves to decorate

Cut up the bacon into small pieces and cook in a saucepan over medium to low heat until the fat is running well but before the bacon starts to crisp. Add the onion, butter and herbs and cook, uncovered, until the onion is really soft. (If the onion is even slightly undercooked, the pâté will sour easily.) Then add the chicken livers over an increased heat and keep turning the mixture until the livers are well cooked but their juices are still somewhat pink.

Liquidise after allowing the mixture to cool a little so that it's safe to handle. You can vary the texture of this by varying the amount of processing – more for a smooth paste, less for chunky. Add the sherry or brandy now, if you like, and perhaps a little pepper. You won't need salt.

The advantage of this recipe is that the saltpetre used in curing the bacon – it is what keeps it pink – will also keep the pâté pink. This takes a couple of days to develop properly, and during this time the potted livers will develop flavour, so you should always try to make the pâté at least two days before you want to serve it.

For the sake of presentation, the newly-made pâté should be turned into a bowl and cling film pressed onto the surface. This stops an unpleasant skin forming. Once the pâté is chilled through, cover it with melted butter to seal and decorate with bay leaves and red peppers. Like this it will keep for well over a week in a refrigerator. Once cut it will keep very well, provided it is not constantly allowed to sit at room temperature when being used.

Red Pepper Mousselines

Serves 6

This pretty vegetable dish can be a starter or a very special accompaniment to a main meal.

1 lb red peppers, sliced
2 oz onions, chopped
½ lb curd cheese
4 beaten eggs
1–2 dsp lemon juice
2 crushed cloves garlic (optional)
Salt and paprika to taste
6 Savoy cabbage leaves, blanched

Cook the peppers and onions in ¼ pint of water. Sieve when cool, and fold in the eggs, cheese and lemon juice. Season to taste with the garlic (if used) and salt. Blanch the cabbage leaves just long enough to soften, and line 6 ramekin dishes with them. Fill with mixture and sprinkle hot or sweet paprika on top.

Bake covered with foil in a tray half-filled with water (a bain-marie) for 30–40 minutes at Gas Mark 2/300°F/150°C. Turn out and serve with some spicy tomato sauce (simply made by reducing the contents of a 14-oz tin of plum tomatoes over heat, with a few dashes of chilli powder or Worcestershire sauce) poured round the mousselines.

Options: Blanched spinach or vine leaves can replace the cabbage.

Chinese Marinated Belly of Pork

Serves 4–12

Hot or cold, this is sensational. It is particularly good served sliced on individual plates of interesting salad leaves – radicchio, spinach and endive, for instance – and then sprinkled with the pan juices or a little dressing.

About 2–2½ lb lean belly of pork with bone
3 tbsp soya sauce
2 tbsp dry sherry or lemon juice
2 tbsp chilli sauce
1 tsp ground allspice
1 tsp ground cinnamon
½ tsp ground cloves
1 crushed garlic clove

Remove the bones from the meat and score through the fat deeply to expose the flesh.

Mix all the marinade ingredients together. Weigh the meat again and put into a shallow dish that will only just hold it, if possible. Pour on the marinade, ensuring it goes into the slashed fat. Turn several times then leave to marinate for up to 24 hours in a refrigerator or just 12 hours in a cool place. Turn the meat from time to time as it suits you. Do not marinate longer than these times, and if you need to do it for less, that is fine, too. Four hours, unrefrigerated, will give quite good results.

Cook on a rack in a roasting pan. First put the meat into a hot oven – Gas Mark 7/425°F/220°C – for 10 minutes, then reduce the heat to Gas Mark 3/325°F/170°C, and cook on for another 30 minutes per pound. If the meat came from the refrigerator, add 5 minutes per pound. Do not baste the meat during cooking.

Once cooked, let the meat rest for 15 minutes, then slice and serve. Serve with a little of the juices that have collected in the base of the pan, defatted if you like. Otherwise let the meat cool, then chill and serve cold.

If the juice has reduced too much at the base of the dish dilute it with a little water to make an amount of tasty sauce.

Slow Baked Mackerel

Serves 4

4 mackerel, 8–12 oz each
½ pint water and wine or water and vinegar mixed
2 tsp mixed pickling spice
1 bay leaf
½ onion, sliced

Lay the cleaned fish in an earthenware dish which will hold them flat without allowing the fish to touch one another. Neither should there be too much extra space. Make up your baking liquid using any two of the three ingredients listed. Half-wine, half-water is rather gentle, half-wine, half-vinegar is more robust. It depends on your palate and the weather. A mixture of cider and cider vinegar is excellent; and do not be afraid to use a red wine or a red wine vinegar for the rosy glow looks good. Do not use malt vinegar.

Pour the liquid over, add pickling spice, bay leaf and onion and cover the dish tightly with foil. Bake for 4 hours at the lowest heat your oven can manage.

Serve hot with a little of the baking liquid. If you are extra clever, pour off the baking liquid, reduce it over fierce heat until rich and highly flavoured, then beat in a few tablespoons of butter. To serve cold, simply remove the onions and spices from the baking liquid then let the fish cool in that. In a refrigerator overnight the liquid will turn to jelly. Serve the fish with some of this, chopped neatly. Horseradish sauce is always good with mackerel; so is apple sauce.

Main Courses and Vegetable Dishes

New Irish Stew

Serves 4–6

It is impossible to make Irish stew the old way unless you use highly flavoured but largely unobtainable mutton. Thus I have given extra savour to today's insipid lamb by adding a little celery and bacon, and by using Guinness instead of the traditional water. What could be more Irish?

2½ lb neck of lamb on the bone
1½ lb large onions
2–3 lb large potatoes
2 celery sticks
6 oz streaky bacon
¾ pint Guinness or stout
Salt and pepper

Halve or quarter the potatoes; peel the onions and slice thickly. Slice the celery finely. Cut the bacon into strips and put into a hot pan until the fat is running well.

Fry the celery and one-third of the onions until brown. Remove. Brown the lamb pieces on both sides. If you like a thicker sauce, first toss the meat in seasoned flour.

Mix the uncooked onion with the cooked bacon, onion and celery. Put into casserole dish in layers with the meat and potatoes, seasoning as you go, with potatoes making the top layer. Pour in the Guinness, cover and simmer on top of the cooker for about 2 hours.

Pork with Coriander and Celeriac

Serves 4

This was one of the year's most popular recipes. Coriander is a warm, orangy spice that is basic to curry. Combined with the fresh taste of knobbly celeriac (celery root) it gives a satisfying taste of the East Mediterranean to pork, although that meat is never eaten in those countries. The Eastern influence is completed by stirring parsley, more coriander, and orange rind into the dish just before serving.

1½ lb lean pork (spare rib or neck end)
8 oz onion, thinly sliced
2 tsp ground coriander
bay leaves, 1 dry
or 2 fresh
12 oz celeriac, peeled and cubed
14-oz tin plum tomatoes
2 tbsp parsley, chopped
1–2 tsp ground coriander
1–2 tsp orange rind, grated
Oil for frying

Cut the pork into large cubes or into evenly sized pieces. Heat a little oil in a large saucepan, then add the pork, onion, coriander, and bay. Cook for 5 minutes or so or until the meat is all sealed and the spice is fragrant, but do not let burn.

Add the celeriac and plum tomatoes, bring to the boil, then cover and simmer for 1½–2 hours. Uncover to reduce if sauce is too thin.

When ready to serve, mix together the parsley, the second amount of coriander and the orange rind. Stir into the saucepan and serve at once with rice or with plain potatoes and any green vegetable that is in season. Spinach is especially good with both coriander and orange.

Option: 1 or 2 chopped cloves of garlic might also be added with the onion.

Chicken with Minted Avocado

Serves 4

The earliest, and still one of the most frequently requested of the recipes I created for the first year of *Breakfast Time.*

3–3½ lb chicken, whole
1 large bunch mint
Juice and rind of 1 lemon
A little butter
1 avocado, ripe
¼ pint double cream

Lay a sheet of foil out on the table. Place the mint under and inside the chicken. Pour the lemon juice over the chicken, and put the lemon rinds inside. Rub pats of butter on top of the chicken, and then wrap it up in the foil, leaving room inside the parcel for steam.

Cook for 1¼–1½ hours at Mark 4/350°F/180°C. Halve the avocado, then cut it lengthwise into thin slices. Pull or slice off the skin, leaving as much of the bright green layer on the flesh as possible. Put into a frying pan over a low heat. Pour the chicken juices over the avocado, stir in the cream, then heat gently for 5 minutes – you need only to heat the avocado through, not cook it. Cut the chicken into four, and arrange the avocado slices nicely. Pour over the sauce, and garnish with a scattering of grated lemon peel or some fresh mint leaves.

The Thatchers' Coronation Chicken

Serves 4–6

This is one of our Prime Minister's favourite recipes, which she was asked to give to *Breakfast Time* just before the 1983 election, as were the other party leaders. Like politics, this one is open to a great many interpretations.

1 cooked chicken, medium size
1 lb approximately mayonnaise
1 dsp apricot jam
1–2 tsp curry paste
¼ pint double cream

The cold cooked chicken should be skinned then pulled into long generous pieces. Do not – ever – chop it or pull it into small pieces as it will look both mean and like yesterday's offering to the cat.

Fold the apricot jam and the curry paste, which will be all the better for being warmed first, into the mayonnaise. This is the amount sold in a large commercial brand's most popular size – don't be tempted to substitute salad cream.

Whip the cream lightly and fold into the flavoured mayonnaise, then turn in the chicken. Chill for a couple of hours and serve with a cold rice salad and a green salad.

Options: Dare I contradict Mrs Thatcher? Well, a little bit, yes. My view is that the apricot jam is a waste of time, and also that the cream is somewhat unnecessary. Instead of the jam use mango, peach or apricot chutney in rather greater quantities than above. And if you can, add a little of the fresh fruit too. You'll find this much more to the modern taste, I think, and will have avoided the addition of cream, which more properly belongs to the next course.

An American Hash

Serves 4–6

Of the many amazing American brunch dishes I discovered at the top of the World Trade Center in New York, this attracted most interest on the programme. Like many traditional American recipes – apple pie in particular! – it is a British dish and essentially a way of reheating and reflavouring cold roasts or other left-over meats. Long slow cooking is the secret.

- 2 lb (generous) cold corned beef, beef or lamb
- 2 lb (generous) cold boiled potatoes
- 1 onion, medium-sized
- 1 dsp green pepper, chopped
- Pepper and nutmeg to taste
- 4–6 dsp butter or dripping
- ¼ pint double cream, stock or water (optional)
- Poached eggs and chilli sauce for topping

All the above proportions may be altered to suit your taste or according to what is available.

First chop the meat quite finely and the potatoes rather roughly. Then chop the onion as finely as possible – mince it if you have a mincer. Mix these three ingredients together with the chopped green pepper, and then flavour generously with black pepper and about ¼ teaspoon of nutmeg, depending on how fresh your stocks are. Melt enough butter or dripping to coat the base of a heavy frying pan, add the mixture and press down rather firmly to compress everything.

Once a crust develops on the bottom turn with a spatula so that most of it is lifted from the bottom, and press down again. Now add the cream, stock or water which helps form a better crust but is not really essential. Cook on slowly, turning from time to time until it looks as though a good half of the mixture has been browned and is well mixed with the portion that has not. Then let the bottom crust get well and truly golden and crisp.

Meanwhile poach some eggs. When they are ready, fold the hash in half in the pan and slide onto a warmed serving dish. Top with the poached eggs – 1 per person – and give a good shake of a medium-hot chilli sauce onto each egg yolk. Serve quickly.

Leekie Pie

Serves 4

This terribly old Welsh-based pie is British cooking at its best – simple but rich. Made with care, it can taste almost like asparagus.

1 lb approximately puff pastry
1 lb leeks, trimmed
1 dsp butter
3 oz streaky bacon
2 large eggs
½ pint cream or milk
Black pepper and nutmeg
Egg for glazing

Slice or chop the leeks very thinly, rinse well and drain. Cook them in a saucepan with no added water until they have wilted and there is no extra free liquid (tilt the saucepan to check). Stir in the butter and let cool.

Line a 9″-diameter pie dish with pastry, leaving enough for a lid, and cut the bacon into thin strips. When the leeks are cool mix them with the bacon and distribute over the pastry. Cover with a pastry topping, decorate if you wish, and ensure you have several large vents cut into the top so that the remaining moisture may escape.

Glaze with beaten egg, then put into a preheated oven Gas Mark 7/ 425°F/220°C: cook for 30 minutes until well-risen and golden brown. Remove from oven. Heat just half of the cream or milk and beat in one of the eggs. Flavour well with freshly ground black pepper and nutmeg. Lift the edge of the pastry or use the vents to pour the mixture over the leeks. Do it slowly. If all has been absorbed, make up another similar mixture and add that. Reduce oven temperature to Gas 4/350°F/180°C and replace pie for 20–25 minutes, which will just set the custard mixture. It doesn't matter if it is a little runny in the middle. Serve the pie warm rather than hot.

Options: The use of cream will give a better set to the pie than the use of milk; and the amount used will depend on the thickness of your dish and of your pastry. Try turning the oven back to the original high heat for a couple of minutes before taking the pie out, to give it a final crispness.

Lentil-Stuffed Cabbage

Serves 4

This vegetarian dish looks like the most beautiful flower when completed. Taken whole to the table as a centrepiece it can be carved and divided as dramatically as you would a Christmas turkey. Either slice it, or simply divide it into four.

3 lb (approx.) savoy cabbage
½ lb carrots, evenly chopped
2 oz onions, thinly sliced or chopped
1 garlic clove (whole, if liked)
1–2 bay leaves
4 oz red lentils
1 tbsp butter
4 tbsp medium oatmeal
1 tsp ground cumin
Salt and pepper
Plain yoghurt and/or tomato sauce to garnish (see recipe)

Simmer carrots, onion, garlic and bay in just ¼ pint of water until as tender or as firm as you like. Add lentils and cook until tender. You may have to add a drop more water, but do not make the mixture too mushy.

Cut off any ragged outside leaves from the cabbage, and trim the stalk-base so that it sits flat. Cut the cabbage almost in four with a large sharp knife, then carefully wash and drain. Steam in a few inches of water in a large saucepan. If the lid does not fit, make a dome of foil. The cabbage should be nicely cooked, but crisp and still green, in 15–20 minutes.

Fry the oatmeal in butter until golden brown. Stir half the oatmeal into the lentil mixture, then flavour with salt, pepper and ground cumin – be quite generous.

Drain the cabbage, then spoon the mixture between the leaves. Take to table scattered with the remaining toasted oatmeal and serve with plain yoghurt, or a sauce made by reducing a 14-oz tin of plum tomatoes over heat, straining, then flavouring with salt, pepper and a little more ground cumin.

Ratatouille

This archetypal summer dish can really be made with any proportion of the main ingredients, but the recipe I like best is the easiest to remember.

1 lb courgettes
1 lb aubergines
1 lb red and green peppers, mixed
½ lb onions
¼ pint olive oil
2 14-oz tins tomatoes
2–3 cloves garlic
Salt and pepper
A little basil and thyme (optional)

Cut the first three ingredients into fairly big pieces, at least 1″ square.

Courgettes and aubergines should be cut so as to have a piece of skin on each bit, which helps the pieces keep their shape. If you like, sprinkle salt on them both after cutting and let them drain for an hour or two, which makes the final dish less robust in flavour – this is not essential. Now slice your onions, then heat the oil in a large pan. Turn all the vegetables into the oil and turn quickly to cover them all with the oil, which is vital for the final flavour. You could get away with using half olive and half another oil, but without the former your ratatouille just won't be good.

Now add the two tins of tomatoes, juice and all. Throw in the cloves of garlic, whole and still in their skins. Leave the lid off and cook gently for at least an hour. If there is still a lot of excess liquid pour it off, reduce over heat to just a few spoonfuls, then pour back into the pan. Only now should you add salt and pepper. If you must have herbs, only a little basil or thyme are useful. Eat ratatouille hot or cold, perhaps sprinkled with a drop more olive oil.

Independence Day Baked Beans

Even though making your own baked beans is as simple as waving a flag, it is just as well to know how to ring the changes with beans bought in a tin. Here are some of the ideas put together by myself and the US Ambassador's wife when she came into the studio.

Boston-style beans

Dissolve ½–1 teaspoon of molasses in a large tinful (14–16 oz) of hot baked beans. A little dried mustard may also be added, plus a little coarse pork sausage or some chunks of bacon or salt pork. Cook until added meat is done.

Richer tomato beans

Add tomato sauce to taste, then spike it up with a dash or two of Worcestershire sauce; tomato purée can be added instead of the tomato sauce (ketchup). Bacon pieces also go well with this.

Chilli beans

Add tomato sauce and a dash of cayenne (chilli pepper) or tabasco.

Chili beans

These are more flavoursome and for this you first add tomato sauce or purée and then *chili seasoning* – note this is spelt with just one 'l' and is a combination of cayenne or chilli pepper plus cumin and other spices. A little garlic or onion juice might also be added.

Red wine beans
For a distinct change, add a teaspoon or more of dried mustard powder to a large tin of beans (14–16 oz size) and then add a medium glassful of red wine and cook gently until the sauce rethickens. Delicious cold or hot. You might also add a bay leaf.

Rice Alternatives

Foreign as it is, rice is very much part of the modern British diet. Yet there are other grain products that are far more delicious, more flexible and, most important, almost impossible to muck up. Indeed, I am convinced that you would have to be very stupid indeed if you could not make a success of these two alternatives to sticky rice.

The first is made from buckwheat, the seed of a grass rather than a grain, and the second is made from precooked wheat. Burghul or bulghur, as it is often called, is actually man's oldest processed food. It is sometimes called cracked wheat, but that is a phrase more accurately used for uncooked grains of wheat that have been cracked under rollers. They would not and could not replace burghul.

Both these grains can either be eaten rather crunchy in the middle or they can be steamed for some time which makes them soft and fluffy. I prefer the former simply for the sake of texture – you may prefer the latter for exactly the same reason!

Each recipe serves from 4–8 or even more, depending on what it is served with and how hungry you are.

Buckwheat Pilaff
½ lb buckwheat — ¾ pint hot water or stock

Brown the buckwheat grains in oil or butter then add the hot water or stock. Let it boil for two minutes, then turn down the heat and simmer very gently until all the liquid has disappeared – just a few minutes is enough. Put a clean cloth over the saucepan and clamp the lid firmly over that. Leave over very low heat for 20–30 minutes – up to a couple of hours if you like – and serve instead of rice.

Options: Chop up about 4 oz bacon into small pieces and fry until the fat is running freely and the bacon is starting to crisp. Add a litle finely chopped onion and/or garlic. Then proceed as above.

An interesting stock is made by reconstituting ¼ oz packet of dried mushroom in ¾ pint water and using that, mushrooms included, to cook the buckwheat.

Burghul Pilaff

½ lb burghul
2 oz butter
½ pint hot water or stock

Lightly brown the burghul in the butter (it must be butter, really), then pour in ½ pint of hot stock or water. Simmer for just long enough to allow the water to be absorbed, then cover the pan with a cloth and clamp on the lid firmly. Leave over a very low heat for 20–30 minutes or until the texture suits you. Serve instead of rice, having added a little salt if needed.

Options: This is wonderful topped with a mixture of raisins, almonds and dried apricots that have been tossed in 2oz of butter. Once the fruit has been put on top, scatter with a little ground cinammon.

Some Potato Recipes

Indian Potatoes

1 lb small potatoes, old or new
1 dsp cumin seeds
2 tbsp ground coriander
½ tsp ground chilli or cayenne

Cook and skin the potatoes. Heat a few tablespoons of oil in a pan and when hot add the cumin seeds. Once they are popping and jumping, stir in the ground coriander and the ground chilli.

Keep stirring for a few seconds until you are sure the spices will not burn, then tumble in the potatoes and turn them in the spiced mixture. Serve when evenly coated and heated through.

Options: Some sliced or flaked almonds make a nice extra addition.

Italian Potatoes Bolognese

1 lb good lean mince
2 inches celery
2 inches carrots, sliced
1-lb tin plum tomatoes
1 or 2 bay leaves
Salt to taste
A quantity of hot cooked potatoes

This delicious bolognese sauce suitable for use on potatoes can of course be used on pasta.

Fry the mince in a little oil together with the celery and carrots which have both been finely cubed. The celery is most important. Once well browned, add all the contents of a 1-lb tin of plum tomatoes in their own juice. Stir well, add a bay leaf or two.

Cook gently for at least 45 minutes or until the meat is tender enough to be squashed against the roof of your mouth with your tongue. Add salt to taste and cook 10 minutes longer. Serve with or without cheese on hot potatoes.

Options: I use neither onions or garlic, but you may add either or both. The real trick is in the long slow cooking for which there is no alternative.

Swedish Roasted Potatoes

Peel the required number of potatoes, which should be evenly sized, then cut a slice from one side so that they sit firmly on their long side or edge. Then, with a very sharp knife and masses of patience, cut about ¾ of the way down towards the base all the way along. You can make the cuts as thick or as thin as you wish.

Melt a little butter in a pan in an oven heated to Gas Mark 7/425°F/220°C. Turn the potatoes in this, then cook for 45 minutes, basting from time to time. They may be finished by sprinkling with a mixture of brown breadcrumbs and grated cheese, or with herb-flavoured butter. Cook an extra 15 minutes depending on size.

Options: You can also use oil which gives a crisper brighter colour, and avoids the cholesterol problem!

Puddings

A Royal Summer Pudding

Serves 4–6

First cousin to the great Russian pudding called kissel and to the Scandinavian rødgrød, this recipe has been adapted from one published by Mrs McKenna, for so long cook to members of the Royal Family. She said her version was a childhood favourite of Prince Charles's. No wonder. It is a thickened summer-fruit jelly and extraordinarily refreshing.

1 lb ripe soft summer fruits
1 pint water
3 dsp cornflour or arrowroot
Sugar to cover
Clotted cream to decorate

As with an English Summer Pudding, the fruits you choose should include red or black currants plus either strawberries, raspberries or blackberries. Use any combination, or if you prefer just one of any of the fruits. Frozen currants and raspberries could be used, too.

Bring the water and the fruit to the boil as slowly as you can, then just simmer for five minutes. Either drain the liquid away through a sieve and discard the pulp, or drain the liquid and then force the cooked fruit through the sieve. There will be little difference to the flavour but the second technique gives a cloudier appearance, and a much bigger yield of course.

Now you need to thicken it, and the exact amount of thickening needed will depend both on the yield and your personal preference; I think it is better if it has rather a wobbly texture. So I use three generous dessertspoons of cornflour or arrowroot mixed in a little water then stirred into the liquid over heat. Cook, stirring constantly until it comes back to the boil, then cook on over a very low heat for another three minutes or so, by which time it will clear and any floury taste will have disappeared.

You *can* add a little sugar now but I don't think you should. Far better to pour the warm pudding into a large bowl, or into individual ones, and then sprinkle generously with caster sugar. This stops an unsightly skin forming.

Chill really well and serve with a little cream and a scattering of more soft fruits. A great splodge of clotted cream, or two of them, will be far more wicked and far more wonderful.

Victoria Plum Ice Cream

Serves 4–6

I still don't understand the enormous success of this recipe – even though the flavour is quite amazing and the technique avoids the problems of making egg custards. It seemed every school-age child in the UK took to it – and woeful you were if *your* mum hadn't made it for you!

1 6.9-oz tin sweetened condensed milk, chilled
¼ pint double cream
1 1¼-lb tin Victoria plums
4 dsp lemon juice or orange juice

Pour the contents of the tin of plums into a large sieve; collect and save the juice. Remove the stones. Force the flesh of the plums through the sieve into another bowl, using the back of a soup ladle or a wooden spoon.

Whip the chilled condensed milk for several minutes until thickened. Add the double cream, and continue beating until thick and light. Lightly stir in the plum purée, and add the lemon juice. Put into a dish and freeze. Reduce the syrup from the can by boiling, and use as a cold sauce for the ice cream, which should be allowed to chill before serving.

Options: Add 1 tsp ground ginger to this mixture. You can make different flavours of ice cream by using about ⅓ pint of other fruit purées.

The Steels' Athol Brose

Serves 4

This ancient Scottish way of ending a meal is doubly delicious if you add that other great speciality of the gardens of Scotland – raspberries. The recipe came from David Steel, Leader of the Liberal Party and a true Scot, so as well as being scrumptious to eat it is authentic.

1 oz medium oatmeal
2 tbsp clear honey
2 tbsp whisky
½ pint double cream
raspberries or blueberries to taste

Toast the oatmeal by tossing and stirring relentlessly in a non-stick pan or in the oven. Let cool. Mix together the honey and the whisky. Whip the cream until firm and peaky but not dry, then fold in the honey-whisky. Leave this to chill. Just before serving, stir in the oatmeal – do it sooner, and it will lose its crunch.

Put raspberries or blueberries – or a mixture – into the bottom of tall glasses or bowls and spoon the Athol Brose over. If you suddenly have more guests, or greedier guests than you expected, it would be better to fold the berries into the mixture.

Gooseberry-Rum Cream

Serves 6

Here apple juice is used to sweeten gooseberries, then vanilla and rum are added to make a new flavour that is perfectly stunning.

1 lb gooseberries, topped and tailed
½ pint apple juice
½–1 tsp vanilla essence
3 tbsp black rum
2 eggs, separated
1 envelope gelatine
¼ pint double cream

Put the gooseberries into the apple juice and simmer gently until the gooseberries are softened – but do not overcook them. Force through a sieve – or liquidise and sieve – and add the vanilla essence and the rum. Whisk the egg yolks into the mixture, then let cool with cling film on the surface to prevent a skin forming. Do not chill.

Melt the gelatine over gentle heat in very little water, then beat into the mixture very well. Whip the cream so that it is firm but not too dry, then fold it in. Whisk the egg whites and fold them in evenly but gently. Ladle the mixture gently into a suitable serving bowl or individual containers. Let set in the refrigerator.

If you prefer to add sugar, add a little to the fruit purée when you add the flavourings. Test the flavour again when the mixture is cool, perhaps after adding the cream, and adjust by adding a touch more vanilla or rum. Remember it will be less sweet when chilled. If you are unconcerned about cholesterol, you can add ½ pint double cream.

Some Strawberry Notes

If you *must* wash strawberries this should be done before the green calyx is removed, otherwise you will rinse away the sugar content. Any washing must be done very quickly under running water (perhaps in a sieve) and the strawberries must be dried as quickly as possible. It absolutely ruins the pleasure of strawberries if they are wet or damp.

The exception to this rule is when they are marinated in a little fruit juice. Orange juice is to be preferred and is one of the best ways to serve strawberries. Do not let them sit in the orange juice for more than ten minutes – there should be just enough to moisten them and to make a nice syrup with a sprinkling of sugar. Of course you can drown the strawberries in fresh orange juice if you are going to eat them directly. A sprinkling of orange-blossom water is marvellous on strawberries. Try flavouring cream for strawberries with orange-flower water or with rose water. Crème de menthe and mint cordial syrups make fabulous dips for strawberries, and chopped or whole mint leaves also make a refreshing, different accompaniment.

Chopped toasted hazelnuts or toasted ground almonds are delicious sprinkled on strawberries, and liqueurs which go well are all the orange ones, chartreuse, coffee and chocolate liqueurs (those made with cream) and kirsch.

Strawberries may also be included in your salads. Or poach small pieces of cucumber lightly, rinse and cool. Mix with sliced strawberries and pour over a light vinaigrette, perhaps made with a nut oil or with a raspberry or strawberry vinegar.

Green ginger root goes very well with strawberries. Either add a little crushed juice (use a garlic crusher) to a vinaigrette or scatter finely diced ginger root over a strawberry and cucumber salad. Strawberries and tomatoes go well together, too – make a salad of the two, use mint leaves for colour and flavour and add a nut oil dressing. If you have no nut oil, use your favourite simple dressing, and add some chopped, toasted hazelnuts or almonds.

Pavlova

Serves 6–8

First let us get one thing straight. A crisp meringue base is not, never was, and never will be a Pavlova. A Pavlova must be crisp on the outside and marshmallow inside – if it ain't, it ain't. Invented in either New Zealand or Australia, depending where you were born, it is as much part of the Australasian scene as kiwis and kangaroos. You certainly could not be born, christened or married without a couple for the guests who are celebrating.

4 large egg whites
8 oz caster sugar
1 tsp vanilla essence
1 tsp vinegar

You may make your Pavlova two ways. Either put the room-temperature egg whites and the sugar all into a bowl at the same time and whisk like mad until good and thick and glossy and peaky. Or whisk the egg whites until stiff, and then whisk in the sugar little by little. Keep on beating until really thick and glossy. Then, whichever path you have followed, beat in the vanilla and the vinegar quickly, making sure it is evenly distributed.

Turn the mixture onto a greased and lightly wetted baking tray and pile into a nice shape (roughly circular with an unsmoothed surface), or line a pie dish of about 8″ diameter with lightly greased foil or greaseproof paper and pile the meringue mixture into that.

Put into an oven that has been prewarmed to Gas Mark ¼/225°F/110°C and cook for 1 hour, then turn off the oven and leave the Pavlova there until cold. If you want it slightly coloured, raise the temperature of the oven a little bit.

Turn out the cold Pavlova. Remove the paper, then invert again so that the crust is on the top. Don't worry about crumbling and cracking as this is essential to the thing.

All Pavlovas should be topped with cream. This may be flavoured with alcohol but should never be sweetened. The most traditional topping would be strawberries smothered with fresh passion-fruit pulp or with slices of fresh kiwi fruit.

An even larger Pavlova would use 6 egg whites and 12 ounces of sugar plus an extra ½ teaspoon each of vanilla and vinegar, and should be cooked for 1½ hours before turning off the oven.

And – just one more time – if it isn't marshmallow in the middle it is not a Pavlova. You can tell them I said so.

Greek Pumpkin Pie

Serves 4–6

This recipe from Northern Greece appealed to me for two reasons: it is a nice change from the usual pumpkin pie, and it makes semolina interesting.

2 lb pumpkin, weighed after peeling and deseeding
2 oz semolina
2–3 oz sugar
2 oz butter
1–2 handfuls currants
8–16 oz pastry, shortcrust or puff
Cinnamon, ground
Allspice, ground
Almonds, flaked

Cook the pumpkin in boiling salted water. Mash or purée the pumpkin, then add the semolina, sugar, butter and currants. This is the basic filling and may be cooked just as it is. Cool before continuing.

Line a suitable tin or dish with ½ lb pastry. Add the filling, then sprinkle generously with cinnamon. Add half this quantity, or less, of ground allspice. If you have some flaked almonds scatter them over the top. If you plan to put an extra ½ lb pastry over the pie, it is best to leave off the almonds as they will go soft underneath.

Start the pie off at a fairly high temperature suitable to the pastry – Gas Mark 7/425°F/220°C for puff pastry, slightly less for shortcrust. Once the pastry is set, turn down to Gas Mark 4/350°F/180°C until the centre is firm and set. If the almonds look as though they may burn, sprinkle or spray them with water.

Serve this pie warm or cold rather than hot, when it is somewhat bland.

Carrot Cheesecake

Serves 6–8

I created this warm, spicy cheesecake to show how delicious low fat, low sugar puddings can be if you try. Older viewers will know that carrot is a traditional British way of sweetening and lightening baked and boiled puddings – especially Christmas puddings.

½ lb gingernut biscuits
1 oz butter, melted
1 lb carrots, trimmed
½ pint orange juice
1 lb cottage, curd or cream cheese
3 tbsp flour
1 tbsp sugar
1 tsp cinnamon, ground
½ tsp nutmeg, ground
½ tsp ginger, ground
3 eggs

Butter lightly an 8-inch spring form pan. Crush the biscuits, then mix well with the melted butter and press well into the base of the spring form, using the back of a spoon to flatten and shape it. Leave to set in a cool place.

Trim the carrots and wash them, but do not peel them unless they are a real mess. Slice thinly and put to cook with the orange juice – about 15 minutes, or until you reckon you can purée them in one way or another.

Once they have formed a nice purée beat in the cheese; if you are using cottage cheese, put it through a sieve first to remove the lumps. Other cheese can simply be beaten a little. Then add all the ingredients to the carrots and cheese mixture and beat really well. If you don't, you will get white lumps where white lumps shouldn't be.

Pour gently into the spring form, then bake for 1 hour at Gas Mark 4/ 350°F/180°C. Leave to cool completely before eating – it is better if left overnight and then chilled slightly.

St Patrick's Bread and Butter Pudding

Serves 6

Invented to mark *Breakfast Time*'s first St Patrick's Day, this wonderful pudding is based on a very old Spanish recipe which I found in Mexico. As St Patrick and all other Irishmen seem inveterate travellers, it appeared suited to adaptation.

10 thick slices white bread, stale
4 oz melted butter
12 oz sugar
1 tsp cinnamon, ground
½ pint Guinness
6–8 oz cottage or curd cheese
Grated peel of 1 orange
2 oz raisins or currants
Nuts for topping (optional)

Cut the crusts from the bread slices and paint well with the melted butter. Lay on a tray and bake in the oven at Gas Mark 6/400°F/200°C until golden and sizzling – check after 5 minutes. Mix together the cinnamon, sugar and Guinness. Simmer in a deep saucepan for 4 minutes. Mix the grated peel into the cheese.

Take a 3–3½-pint ovenproof dish and layer the ingredients. Start with the baked and buttery toast, then add the cheese, raisins or currants, and some of the syrup. Finish with a layer of toast and pour on the remaining syrup. Sprinkle on the nuts, if used, and leave for 10 minutes. Bake at Gas Mark 4/350°F/180°C for 20 minutes until the toasts are swollen and the top layer has crispened.

Black Cherry Oven Pancake

Serves 4

Nothing beats this for a spectacular but simple pudding. It's really a sweet Yorkshire Pudding, I suppose – so be certain the oven and the baking dish are as sizzling hot as possible.

Batter:

3 oz plain flour
¼ pint milk
2 eggs

Sauce:

1-lb tin pitted black cherries, drained with juice reserved
4 tbsp butter
3 dsp black rum or brandy
3 dsp brown sugar

Make the batter by beating the eggs into the flour and adding the milk gradually. Preheat the oven to maximum temperature. Put the sauce ingredients into a pan or dish of 10-inch diameter, and place in the oven until very hot and bubbling.

Quickly add the batter and bake for 15 minutes. Meanwhile, heat the juice from the cherries until reduced by half. Serve the pancake with the hot cherry syrup and cream – perhaps with a little more rum?

Upside-down Orange-Caramel Apple Pie

Serves 2–6, depending on Greed Factor

One of the most amazing Gosh Factors of the year was my visit to the Royal Horticultural Society's Apple and Pear Show, where I learned that there are more than 600 varieties of apples grown in this country. But what do we get in the shops? . . . about 6 types.

Apple pies are a great star of British cooking but don't be inhibited and use only Bramleys. Cox's Orange Pippins make fabulous baked pies and sponges and need no added sugar. And Golden Delicious are just right for my version of a famous upside-down French apple tart. I know the name is a bit of a mouthful, but I promise you will never have quite such delicious mouthfuls.

½ lb puff pastry
2 oz butter
2 oz white or demerara sugar
1 small orange
2 lb or more Golden Delicious apples
1 oz sugar
1–2 oz butter

Put 2 oz butter, sugar and the juice of the orange into a small pan and cook until a deep golden-brown colour without letting it burn. Turn the liquid into a deep baking dish of 8″-10″ diameter. Segment the apples, then core and peel them. Do not slice thinly, but leave in generous segments. Arrange neatly atop the caramel, sprinkling with the sugar. Dot the 1–2 oz butter evenly over the top.

Roll out the pastry and let it rest a few minutes to regain its shape. Roll around your pin, then place on top of the pie. Turn the edge back on itself and, if you have extra pastry, make yet another layer around the rim. The pastry does not have to be very neat as it will be turned upside-down when the dish is cooked. Place into a preheated oven at Gas Mark 6/400°F/200°C for about 30 minutes, or until the pastry is well risen and golden brown. Let stand a few minutes, then put a plate on the top and quickly invert. Serve warm rather than hot, with lots of cream.

Options: If you like a strong orange flavour with apple, and I do, you could grate the peel of the orange over the apple or roll it into the puff pastry, perhaps with some added butter.

Bread and Baking

Wholemeal or Wholewheat Loaf

Wholemeal and wholewheat are exactly the same thing; it is wheatmeal which is an extraction flour – usually only 81 per cent or 85 per cent of the whole grain. The name wheatmeal will no longer be allowed to be used when the new flour legislation is introduced in 1984.

Remember that in all bread recipes you should have everything warm, including the flour and the tins, and that only dried yeast requires sugar to make it work. When the dough is left to rise it must be in a warm, *not* hot place. And when in doubt about amounts of yeast – especially dried yeast – always use less rather than more. Too much yeast, or dough which has risen too quickly, will give a dry, fast-staling bread.

The most popular wholemeal recipe seems to be the non-knead loaf, and the best-known recipe for this is the so-called Grant Loaf. I'll give you that first, and then follow it with some of the many variations viewers have sent in.

Grant Loaf

To make three loaves

3 lb wholemeal flour – stoneground is best
2 pints lukewarm water
1 oz fresh yeast or ½ oz dried yeast
2–3 tsp dark brown sugar (muscovado)
4 tsp sea salt

Warm the flour. Crumble the fresh yeast, and pour on about ½ pint water and leave in warm place until frothy. If using dried yeast, add a pinch or two of the sugar. Dissolve remaining sugar and salt in the remaining 1½ pints of water. Grease 3 2-pint bread tins and keep warm. When the yeast is ready, make a well in the centre of the flour, pour in the yeast and then the liquid. Mix well by hand. The dough should be fairly soft, rather like a scone mixture. Add extra water or flour if you think it's necessary. Put into tins, cover with a damp cloth and let it rise well. Remember that wholemeal bread will not rise an extra amount in the oven. The bread should be over the edge of the tin if you use the above size. Bake in pre-heated oven at Gas Mark 6/400°F/200°C for approximately 40 minutes.

To get a nice crust, turn the loaf out of tin before it is fully cooked and finish on rack. Tap the bottom with your knuckles; if you hear a good hollow sound, the bread is done.

To make one loaf, use about 1 lb flour, about ¾ pint water and ½ oz fresh yeast, 1 tsp sugar and 1 heaped tsp salt.

Options: Longer lasting qualities are obtained with the addition of a little fat or egg to a loaf. Both these give a more cake-like texture if used in excess, and also tend to make the bread heavier. In the above recipe I would use no more than a few fluid ounces of milk or a couple of ounces of butter or fat for 3 lb of flour. Molasses can also be used instead of the brown sugar, and other viewers have used honey, which is very nice indeed. You can also replace some of the flour with white flour to make a slightly lighter loaf.

Some viewers said they always knead their wholemeal dough; you can, of course, but this is considered by some authorities to diminish the nutritive value of the bread. If you have more than 25 per cent white flour, then you should knead it a little.

Vitamin C Wholemeal Bread

The use of Vitamin C to give a good rise is increasingly popular. It will help wholemeal breads, but is really more useful in white breads as it eliminates the need for a second rising. Here is a sample recipe – without the benefit of the Vitamin C tablet to strengthen the flour's protein the fat added would make this somewhat heavy. There is no dietary benefit in the Vitamin C tablet as this is destroyed by the heat of the baking.

1½ lb stoneground wholemeal flour
1 25-mg Vitamin C tablet
½ oz fresh yeast, or half as much dried yeast and a pinch of sugar
¾ pint (approx.) warm water
1 tbsp sea salt
1 tbsp dark brown sugar or molasses
½ oz butter, lard or margarine.

Warm the flour. Dissolve the Vitamin C tablet and the yeast (and pinch of sugar if using dried yeast) in a little of the warm water and leave in a warm place for 10–15 minutes, covered. Dissolve the salt, sugar and fat in the remaining water. Make a well in the flour, add the yeast mixture, and then the flavoured water. Mix well, and knead if you like for 5–10 minutes (I wouldn't, personally). Divide into two and put into 2 greased and warmed 1-lb tins. Cover with a damp cloth and leave to rise in a warm place. Bake at Gas Mark 7/425°F/220°C for 35–40 minutes.

Note: You will need a different amount of water/liquid each time you make such breads (*any* bread in fact). Get to know the texture to aim for and make that each time.

Mixed Grain Breads and Mixed Flour Breads

Many people add a number of grains and seeds to the outside of bread before baking – sesame seeds seem the most popular. Simply sprinkle the inside of the prepared tins before you add the dough. The following rather chewy bread adds kibbled wheat, coarsely cracked wholewheat grains, to the dough. Soak as suggested or, for a less rugged texture, simmer whole wheat grains (not kibbled) until soft; drain off the cooking water. Here is the original recipe sent to *Breakfast Time.*

Kibbled Wheat Bread

- 3 lb wholemeal flour
- 2 cups kibbled wheat
- 1 pint boiling water and ½ pint lukewarm water
- 1 oz fresh yeast or ½ oz dried yeast and a pinch of sugar
- 1 dsp sea salt
- 2 tbsp honey

Cover the kibbled wheat with the boiling water and leave until just lukewarm. Warm the wholemeal flour, add the sea salt. Crumble the fresh yeast (or the dried yeast plus a pinch of sugar) into ½ pint of lukewarm water. Once frothy – after about 10 minutes – stir in the honey. First add the yeast mixture to the soaked grains, then the flour. Mix very well, then knead a little to ensure a good even texture. Divide into two and put into 2 8-inch loaf tins. Cover with a damp cloth and stand in a warm place for about 40 minutes until approximately doubled in bulk.

Bake at Gas Mark 6/400°F/200°C for ¾–1 hour.

Combination Breads

Perhaps the most popular recipes were those that combined wholemeal and white flour. There is no rule about proportions, and almost no two people used the same. Some used 1 lb wholemeal to ½ lb of white flour – others simply added a handful or so of one to the other. No combination will be bad. It's all a matter of what you like. The more white flour you get, the lighter the loaf will be in colour and texture, and provided you are using proper bread flour – it must say *strong* white flour – you will get a better rise. Bread with a good proportion of white flour is improved by being allowed to rise twice before baking, but the use of a Vitamin C tablet dispenses with this. The following recipe was sent in by 70-year-old Mrs Opie of Falmouth, and is typical of the loaves that seem a great British favourite.

1 lb stoneground wholemeal flour
½ lb strong white flour
½–¾ oz fresh yeast (less is better)
½ pint cold water mixed with
¼ pint boiling water

1½ tsp salt
1 tsp sugar
1½ oz butter

Warm the mixed flours. Crumble the yeast into a little of the water. Mix the salt, sugar and butter into the rest of the water and keep warm. When the yeast is working, make a well in the flour, pour in the yeast mixture, and then the water. Mix well with your hands, turn out onto a floured board and knead for about 10 minutes until the dough is no longer sticky. Replace the dough in the bowl. Cover with a damp cloth and leave in a warm place until it has doubled in bulk. Knock down the dough, knead for just a minute or two, then divide into two portions. Divide between two warmed and greased tins, cover again, and let rise once more. Bake at Gas Mark 6/400°F/200°C for 40 minutes, moving to a lower shelf half-way through. Remove from tins and return to the oven for a few minutes until the bottom is crisp and the loaves give a hollow sound when tapped.

Bran-Plus Loaf

Bran is a common additive to bread doughs – it can be added to any bread dough you like for extra nutty flavour and for even more roughage. This recipe is a fairly typical one. I think I might use a little less yeast, and it is probably worth trying a Vitamin C tablet in this one. . . but here is the recipe as sent by Mrs Heeley who says it is foolproof and a guaranteed success for even the biggest culinary idiot!

2 lb stoneground wholemeal flour
3 oz bran
1 oz wheatgerm (optional)
1 tsp molasses, honey or brown sugar
1 oz fresh yeast or ½ as much dried yeast and a pinch of sugar
1 dsp sea salt
(up to) 1½ pints tepid water.

Mix together the flour, bran, wheatgerm and salt, and warm thoroughly. Mix the yeast with about ¼ pint water and leave for 10–15 minutes in a warm place to work. Mix honey, molasses or sugar into the remaining water. Once all is ready, mix everything together and knead for no longer than 5 minutes. Put into 2 greased and warmed 2-pint tins and cover with a damp cloth. Leave in a warm place until well risen. Bake in a preheated oven as in the previous recipe.

Oatmeal Bread from 'Laurel's Kitchen'

This recipe was sent in by an American. Oatmeal bread is chewy with a delicious sweetness. The addition of wheatgerm and dried skimmed milk make it very healthful. It toasts terribly well, too. You can add a little oatmeal to any bread recipe, but here is what Beth Vinsand recommends. A cup is the equivalent of the 8 fl oz measure in your measuring jug:

3 cups medium to coarse oatmeal
2 tbsp cooking oil
2 fl oz honey
1 tbsp salt
½ cup wheatgerm (toasted is best)
3 cups boiling water
1 tbsp dried yeast, and a pinch of sugar
5–5½ cups wholemeal flour
2 oz dried skimmed milk powder

Put the oats, oil, honey, salt and wheatgerm into a large bowl and pour on the boiling water. Let it cool to lukewarm. Then dissolve the yeast in a little warm water and a pinch of sugar. Mix the flour and milk powder together and warm them. Once the yeast is working, add it to the oat mixture and stir. Then mix in the flour/milk mixture, cup by cup until you have a good stiff dough. Turn on to a floured board and knead just long enough to ensure that the mix is even. Put the dough into a greased bowl, cover with a damp cloth then let it rise in a warm place until doubled in bulk. Punch it down, form into two loaves and place seam-side down in warmed, greased loaf tins. Cover and let rise until doubled. Bake in a pre-heated oven at the same temperature as the last two recipes, for about 45 minutes.

White Breads

Home-made white bread is a revelation. It has flavour and texture quite unlike any that can be bought. The secrets of making all white bread are simple. You must knead really well; the dough must rise at least twice; and the longer it takes for each rise to happen the better the flavour will be. Always use less rather than more yeast: ½ oz of fresh yeast or ¼ oz of dried will raise a dough made with 2 lb flour admirably. Only when you start to use 3 lb of flour do you need to consider using 1 oz of yeast. Dough can be popped into the refrigerator to slow it down and can even be left there all night. Remember that you are in charge of bread dough. Although it is a long time between mixing the dough and baking it, your attention is only required for about 20 minutes. The rest of the time the dough is getting on by itself without any help from you, or any need of it. And if you find you want to speed things up a little then put the dough somewhere warmer. Lots of people said they put it out in the garden beside them so they could keep an eye on it. Fine – but it must not be too hot or the fast rise will give a nasty texture. If you really can't wait for a second rise, then use a Vitamin C tablet and put the kneaded dough directly into pans and bake when it has doubled in bulk.

Basic White Loaf

2 lb strong white flour
1 rounded tbsp sea salt
½ oz fresh yeast, or half as much dried and a pinch of sugar
¾–1 pint warm water, perhaps with a few tbsp milk added or including up to 1 oz butter, lard or fat

Mix together the flour and salt and warm through. Crumble the yeast into a little of the water and leave in a warm place for 10–15 minutes until frothing well. Mix the yeast liquid well, then pour into a well in the warmed flour. Mix in the warm water until a firm dough is obtained. Turn out and knead very well, adding more flour or water until you have a dough that will not stick to the hands. Knead until the texture changes and the surface of the dough is as smooth as satin. Replace in a clean warm bowl, cover with a damp cloth and leave until doubled in bulk.

Knock down and knead another minute or two, then form into rolls or loaves, let double in bulk again and bake in a hot oven, Gas Mark 8/450°F/230°C for about 1 hour for a large loaf, and 40–50 minutes for smaller.

Note: To glaze this bread, either paint with beaten egg before baking, or, for a matt finish, rub over with butter when just from the oven.

Vienna Loaf

Although the version of this recipe that was sent to me used an 85 per cent flour, you could use white (strong white) flour, too.

1 lb 85 per cent flour
1 tsp sea salt
½ oz fresh yeast or half as much dried and a pinch of sugar
½ pint warm milk
2 tsp dark brown or golden granulated sugar (maximum amount)
1½ oz butter
1 medium egg
1 25-mg Vitamin C tablet
Beaten egg to glaze
Cracked wheat to decorate if you want, or poppy seeds

Warm the flour and salt together in a large bowl. Add the yeast to 1 inch of milk and leave to work. Melt the sugar and butter in the rest of the warm milk, beat in the egg, crumble in the Vitamin C tablet, and ensure that it is dissolved.

Mix everything together to form a firm dough and knead for 5–7 minutes, adding extra milk or flour as necessary. Too soft a dough will mean the bread spreads out too much. Form into two loaves; the Vienna shape is a torpedo, somewhat narrower at both ends. Cover and leave to rise on a baking tray in a warm place, until doubled in bulk. Once ready to bake, brush with beaten egg and sprinkle with cracked wheat or, if using white flour, with poppy seeds.

Bake at Gas Mark 8/450°F/230°C for about 20 minutes. Cool on wire rack.

Here are two interesting variety breads sent in by *Breakfast Time* enthusiasts:

Cheese Bread

½ oz fresh yeast
5–6 fl oz lukewarm water or water and milk
12 oz strong white flour
½ tsp salt
½ oz butter or lard
4 oz grated strong cheddar
1 oz very finely chopped onion, spring onion or chives
¼ tsp dried mixed herbs or oregano
Beaten egg to glaze

Dissolve the yeast in a little water. Sift the flour and salt, rub in the butter or lard, then add the cheese, onion and herbs. Make a well and mix in the yeast and the remainder of the water. Mix to form a good elastic dough. Knead until smooth and leave to double in bulk under a damp cloth in a warm place. Divide the dough into three even pieces, shape each into a 12″ roll, then plait them together. Put onto a baking tray, cover and leave until doubled in bulk. Brush with egg and scatter with a little more grated cheese. Bake at Gas Mark 6/400°F/200°C for 20–25 minutes.

Beer Bread

3 cups self-raising flour
3 tbsp sugar
12 fl oz lager at room temperature
2 oz melted butter (optional)

Quickly mix together the flour, sugar, melted butter if used, and lager. Put into a greased, warm loaf tin. Bake for 45 minutes at Gas Mark 4/350°F/180°C.

Irish Wheaten Bannocks

The second-most favourite recipe sent in was for wheaten bannocks which are really a sort of enriched, wholemeal scone mixture. Traditionally these are made with buttermilk and baking soda but as the former is not easily available I suggest you use ordinary milk and baking powder.

½ lb wholemeal flour
2 dsp plain flour
1½ tsp baking powder
½–1 tsp salt
2 oz butter or margarine
1 beaten egg
½ pint warmed milk

Mix together the dry ingredients, then rub in butter or margarine. Mix in the beaten egg and warmed milk quickly. Turn out onto a floured board and tumble quickly and lightly a few times to even out the mixture, then turn into a floured sandwich tin. Pat lightly into a round shape, then mark into quarters. Bake in a preheated oven at Gas Mark 5/375°F/190°C for 30 minutes. Turn out on to a cooling tray and cover with a cloth. The egg and butter make this quite a heavy mixture, so spread with lashings of butter. They are also very good toasted.

Hot Cross Buns

To make 12

Spicy and heavy, the texture of these buns is an authentic reminder of how dreadfully unreal modern versions can be. The high proportion of yeast used here means they stale easily – but then they are even better for toasting. You can't lose!

1 lb strong white flour
1 oz fresh yeast or ½ oz dried yeast and a pinch of sugar
½ pint milk
2 tsp salt
½ oz sugar
2 oz light brown or demerara sugar
2 oz butter, chopped
1 egg, beaten
2 oz mixed peel
2 tsp mixed spice
4 oz currants

Put the flour to warm in the oven. Warm the milk. Dissolve the yeast (or dried yeast and pinch of sugar) in half the milk and leave in a warm place for about 10 minutes. In the rest of the milk put the salt, sugar, butter, beaten egg, peel and mixed spice. Leave until the butter is melted.

Make a well in the warmed flour. Strain the yeast mixture into the other liquid, then gradually work these into the flour. You may have to add extra flour; but make a dough that is soft and slightly sticky to the touch. Knead gently until it is smooth and even in texture. Now work in the currants, trying not to crush them too much. Put into a lightly oiled bowl, cover with cling film and let rise in a warm (not hot) place for 2 hours or until doubled in bulk. If you let the dough get too cool the butter will set, if too hot the egg will – and both will prevent a good rise.

Knock the dough down, and using a sharp knife cut into 12 even pieces, form into rolls and arrange evenly on a floured tray. To make a cross, either cut one with a sharp knife now, or make the following paste:

For the crosses:

3 tbsp plain flour | 2 tbsp milk

Mix well, adding extra flour if necessary until firm enough to roll out thinly. Cut into thin strips and decorate the rolls. You can do this at this stage or after the rolls have rested and risen. Cover the formed rolls with a light, damp cloth and let rise until doubled in bulk – perhaps 45 minutes. Bake in a preheated oven Gas Mark 4/350°F/180°C for 15 minutes or until well-risen and golden brown.

For the glaze:

2 tbsp milk | 2 tbsp sugar

Boil together for 1 minute and paint onto the buns the moment they come out of the oven.

Serve warm now, or cut and toast the next morning.

Quick Scones

To make 6–8

As with bread making the secret of nice, light scones is to have all the ingredients warm – the oven must be preheated and the baking tray should be heated in the oven whilst you are making the mixture. The exact proportion of milk to flour is impossible to give, as flour changes in its ability to absorb liquid depending both on the brand and on the weather. The basic recipe I have always used is to add 1 generous teaspoon of baking powder, a pinch of salt and a teaspoon or so of sugar, depending on how sweet you like them, to every heaped cup of plain flour. The cup used should be fairly big, and the flour should only be slightly warmed.

Mix the dry ingredients together for a two-cups-of-flour mixture, warm a generous ½ pint of milk, and then work quickly to mix that in to make a light soft dough. You may need more milk – or you might need more flour if the mixture is too sloppy.

Tip the mixture out on to a floured surface then as lightly as possible knock it gently into an oblong shape – do not tap or pat the top as this will knock out the air. Then use the sharpest knife you have to cut the scone mixture into squares. The use of pastry cutters should be avoided as this presses the mixture down and makes them flatter. Use extra flour if the mixture is slightly too sticky to cut (professionals recommend you use an old-fashioned razor blade rather than a knife). Take the tray from the oven, sprinkle generously with flour, then quickly arrange the scones on the hot tray. Use a palette knife or egg slice to avoid handling the scones themselves.

Bake undisturbed at Gas Mark 7/425°F/220°C for 15–20 minutes according to how big you made them. Let them cool on a rack – cover with a clean cloth if you like them to be somewhat soft. Do not cut open, but pull apart. Because these do not contain butter they need to be eaten quickly.

Options: Once you have perfected your scone-making technique you may like to flavour them. Some of the best are the simplest, and to two cups of flour you might like to add ½–1 teaspoon of vanilla essence and the grated rind of a large orange, or 6 or more generous tablespoons of desiccated coconut. The latter is especially delicious if the coconut is toasted in the oven first.

Bounty **Banana Pilhi**

Serves 6–8

An old family recipe from Pitcairn Island. Pilhi was supposedly invented by my *Bounty* mutineer ancestors and their Tahitian wives to replace Yorkshire Pudding. In fact, except for the flour, it is an authentic Tahitian dish of great antiquity. Serve it hot with all roasts, or enjoy it cold as a snack.

2 lb bananas, very ripe
4 oz desiccated coconut
2 oz plain flour
½ tsp salt

Mash the bananas and stir in the coconut, flour and salt. Turn into buttered dish, so that the mixture is at least 1″ thick.

Bake at Gas Mark 4/350°F/180°C for 60 minutes or until crisp and golden brown on top, and set in the middle.

The Nettles' Carrot and Banana Cake

For one 8″ × 8″ square cake

The Nettle family became national TV stars when they allowed Diana Moran, our Green Goddess, to get them into shape. As a reward for their hard work *Breakfast Time* gave them a cake – but a low fat, high fibre one created by me. Believe me, it is good enough to start you dieting.

1 lb wholewheat flour
1 tsp baking soda
2 tsp baking powder
1 tsp allspice, ground
1 tsp nutmeg, ground
½ tsp cloves, ground
12 oz carrots, trimmed but not peeled unless very old
1lb (before peeling) very ripe bananas
4 eggs
½ pint low fat yoghurt or skimmed milk
4 tbsp sunflower or safflower oil
4 tbsp clear honey
3 tsp vanilla essence

Mix the dry ingredients and spices together. Grate the carrots and bananas, mix well, then toss in the flour mixture. Beat together the eggs and the remaining ingredients. Stir into the flour/carrot mixture as lightly as possible.

Turn into the cake tin, which should be oiled. Even if it has a non-stick surface, it is also advisable to line it with greaseproof paper or the wrapping from butter or margarine. Bake in a preheated oven Gas Mark 3/325°F/170°C for about 1½ hours. Test with a skewer or sharp knife to see if it comes out clean.

Festive Banana Cake

For a 9″–10″ cake tin

My childhood favourite – indeed this is as basic to growing up in New Zealand as fish and chips are in the UK.

6 oz butter
9 oz caster sugar
3 medium eggs
3 medium to large ripe bananas
3 tbsp milk
1 tsp vanilla essence
3 rounded tsp baking powder
12 oz plain flour

Preheat the oven to Gas Mark 3/325°F/170°C and lightly flour a 9″–10″ deep cake tin (not necessarily a non-stick type).

Cream the butter and sugar together specially well, then beat in the eggs one at a time. Mash the bananas to a froth (use only those that are really ripe, with a mottled skin). Stir in the milk and vanilla. Sift together the baking powder and the flour.

Mix in the banana mixture and the flour to the eggs alternately, but do not over-beat. Pour into the tin, and bake for 40–60 minutes according to the size of the tin. Test with a skewer or sharp knife to see if it comes out clean. Cool for 10 minutes as it is, then turn the cake out onto a wire rack and leave until fully cool.

Options: It is delicious eaten just like this, but there are two ways to dramatise the banana flavour. Either split the cake and fill it with a mixture of mashed banana, a little orange or lemon juice and some whipped cream; or make a Chocolate Banana Icing. Mash a nice ripe banana into 1 lb of icing sugar, then gradually add softened butter until you get a nice spreading consistency. It takes but a second in a food processor. Then add cocoa powder, generously, until you have a rich chocolate colour and flavour. Don't use drinking chocolate powder. Spread over the top and sides of the cake, leave the icing rough, and let it set before serving. Of course, you could both fill it *and* ice it.

Rough Puff Pastry

John Tovey of the famed Miller Howe Hotel in Cumbria taught me this. It's virtually foolproof, provided you use strong (breadmaking) flour.

For 1lb of pastry:

½ lb strong plain flour
A small pinch of salt
¼ lb soft margarine or butter
¼ lb soft American lard, or other shortening
½ tbsp lemon juice made up to ¼ pint with very cold water

Sieve the flour into a large bowl and add a pinch of salt. Then add the fats in ½-oz pieces. Mix lightly, then make a well in the centre. Pour the lemon juice/water mixture into this and mix coarsely with a palette knife.

Scrape all the mixture out onto a large floured rolling area. Shape this mixture into a brick shape, the shortest end nearest you. Holding the rolling pin very delicately, gently roll the brick out, away from you, to make a long rectangle of about 16″ × 5″. Fold this into three, the third nearest you over the middle third, and the further third over these two. Gently tap closed the open sides of this dough 'parcel'.

Give the dough one quarter turn so that the long seam facing you is now turned to be on your left-hand side. Allow it to rest for one minute. Repeat this procedure three times, giving one quarter turn each time. Try not to force the dough, even if it gradually loses its original rectangular shape. Chill before rolling out to the shape you desire.

Bake in a hot oven, Gas Mark 8/450°F/230°C.

Choux Pastry

To make about 24 medium choux buns

½ pint water	5 oz plain strong white flour
4 oz butter	A pinch salt
1 oz white sugar (for sweet pastry only)	4 eggs

For glaze

1 egg yolk	A little water

Measure ½ pint boiling water and put into a saucepan. Add the butter and leave over very low heat until it is all melted. Then turn up the heat until the liquid boils. As soon as it does, pour in the sieved flour and salt all at once. If making sweet choux pastry, dissolve the white sugar in the boiling water before adding the flour and salt. Remove from heat and stir just enough to blend everything and until it forms a ball that comes away from the side of the pan. Leave over low heat, turning gently for about half a minute. Do not beat at this stage. Let it cool to lukewarm.

Now slowly beat in the eggs one by one, ensuring that the mixture is smooth and even before adding the next. This can take a little effort and is better if done with mechanical assistance. In humid weather or kitchens, or for a crisper choux pastry, use small eggs or cut down the number to 3 or even 2. The final texture should be like a smooth, glossy, thick batter.

Always cook choux pastry on a wet surface as the steam helps it rise. The simplest way to shape the pastry is by piping it, but the use of teaspoons or dessertspoons will give equally good results – indeed I prefer the rather more ragged results this method gives. To make evenly shaped choux buns you could pipe or pile the paste into metal patty tins which, like baking trays, should be slightly damp. You can also simply make a big ring of choux pastry on a damp baking sheet and cook that. Paint on the glaze quickly.

Place the choux shapes into a preheated oven, Gas Mark 6/400°F/200°C until well risen, crisp and golden brown. This will take from 15–25 minutes, depending on the size. Don't peep for the first 5 minutes! Take out the trays, make a small incision at the side of each piece and return to the oven at its lowest heat until dried out – about 10 minutes. A large ring of choux pastry might take up to 40 minutes to cook and would need a longer drying-out period.

Once cooled, cut open and remove any excess uncooked pastry. For best effect do not cut the buns or éclair shapes in half horizontally, but at an angle from the top to the opposite side of the bottom.

Fillings

The most popular fillings are whipped cream flavoured with vanilla and sugar, with sugar and rosewater, or with rum. It is also good to combine whipped cream with vanilla-flavoured chestnut purée – about equal quantities is right. Enhance this further by adding black rum.

Filled choux buns or profiteroles can be piled simply into a tower to make a party centrepiece, and they can also be formed into more interesting shapes by being stuck together with caramel. This is simply made by melting sugar over heat until golden brown. Keep this slightly warm and use a spoon to dab the liquid sugar onto each bun to join it to the next. Use great care as the sugar is exceptionally hot. You can make a tapered tower by constructing it around a cone called a *croquembouche* mould.

Otherwise, make a battlement or circle of the filled pastries on a large platter, again using the liquid sugar to stick them together. A ring made into a crown shape looks wonderful if it is filled with such soft fruits as raspberries and strawberries.

For added colour, dab a small piece of cherry or strawberry onto the exposed filling of each pastry.

Toasted Almond Pastry

Makes approximately 1 lb

This may be used for any fruit pie or, with a touch of added sugar, can be baked in fingers as a quick and delicious accompaniment to simple puddings of ice cream, fruit etc.

2 oz toasted ground almonds
8 oz plain soft flour (not bread flour)
1 oz sugar – caster is best
5–6 oz salted butter
1 egg
Cold water

To toast the almonds, toss or stir them carefully in a non-stick pan over medium heat. Ensure that they are evenly brown and beware of burning, which happens easily. As soon as they look right, tip them out into a flat plate as the heat of the pan will continue to cook and brown them past the stage you want.

Mix the flour, almonds and sugar, plus a touch of salt if you like – I think using salted butter adds enough salt. The butter should be very firm. Chop it into small pieces. Quickly toss in the flour to coat each piece of butter, then chop into smaller pieces with a knife. Continue rubbing the butter into the flour, keeping the amount you are working with high above the bowl and dropping it back from that height as this helps keep the mixture cool. Do not rub until the mixture is even but continue only until most of it looks like rather coarse breadcrumbs. Some large flakes of butter actually help make a light pastry.

Lightly beat the egg and stir it in with a knife. Then gradually add very cold water – just a few good splashes is all that is needed. Turn with the knife until the mixture, although crumbly, is starting to stick together and a small amount will cohere if squeezed. Turn out and pat into shape very lightly, then wrap in cling film and chill for 30–40 minutes, which helps consolidate the mixture. Roll out lightly on a floured board and use as any other short pastry.

The Store Cupboard

Summer Bounty

Once summer comes, the UK abounds with delicious possibilities for making next winter more fun. One of the simplest is to make fruit-flavoured spirits and liqueurs which will be ready by Christmas and last much longer – if you make enough.

There are no hard-and-fast rules about making your own fruit-flavoured alcohols and liqueurs. But before you start you must decide if you are going to make a sharp brandy-style drink or a sweeter liqueur-style drink.

In general you will find that for each 1 lb weight of berry fruits such as raspberries, strawberries, blackcurrants, you should use 1 pint of alcohol – brandy, gin, vodka or whisky. The flavour will be enhanced by anything up to 4 oz of sugar. But to make a liqueur you should use 12 oz of sugar per pint of alcohol: start with less if you fear for your figure or your sweet tooth.

Never crush the fruit, but if you are using something with a tough skin, like damsons or sloes, then either prick them or cut into thick slices.

Put the fruit into a clean jar with a firm top, layering with sugar. Then pour on the brandy, gin, vodka or whisky. Keep in a cool place and give it a few turns every day for a couple of weeks until the sugar has dissolved. Keep for 2 or 3 months to get maximum results before use.

Serve the alcohol chilled as an aperitif: serve the sweeter liqueurs after a meal. Both make fabulous additions to a glass of champagne, especially the liqueurs. And of course, fruit such as peaches, raspberries, blackberries and blackcurrants, impregnated with liqueur, give a fabulous lift to all kinds of puddings – even humble ice cream.

To make smaller quantities, simply divide the recipe: i.e. ½ lb of fruit and ½ pint of your chosen liquor. But don't worry – you can add a little more or a little less of anything without a disastrous result. I think the greatest flavour I made in 1983 came from soaking English blueberries in gin. Unlike most fruits, these keep their colour wonderfully. At Christmas time I entertained some cold Americans with small glasses of chilled Blueberry Gin, then a few days later served some of the *Breakfast Time* staff hot gammon sprinkled with the gin-soaked berries. Everyone was as excited as if I had spent £100 a head.

Elderflower Champagne

2–3 large heads of elderflowers – dusty with pollen
1¼ lb sugar
2 tbsp white wine vinegar
juice and rind of 1 lemon (optional)

Place the elderflowers in a gallon of cold water with the sugar and vinegar, adding the juice and rind of a lemon if liked.

Leave in a cool place for 24 hours, then strain into screw-topped bottles (they *must* be screw-topped) and leave for two weeks in a cool, dark place.

It can be left for a total of six months, but no longer.

Elderflower Fritters

4–5 elderflower heads
4 oz plain flour
1 tsp baking powder
1 egg
1 tsp sugar
½ pint milk

Make the batter mixture by sieving the flour with the baking powder. Make a well in the centre and beat in the egg. Add the milk gradually, beating all the time. Stir in the sugar, and then put in the elderflower heads. Leave to stand for ½ hour to let the flavour develop.

Cook as for Scotch pancakes: fry in a little melted butter, a large spoonful at a time, and serve with squeeze of lemon or orange juice.

Spicy Pickled Peaches

For 1 lb of peaches

Whether you want to eat them immediately on summer picnics, or save to serve with cold meats in winter, pickled summer fruits are a wonderful standby that even the most inexperienced can make.

1 lb peaches, ripe but firm
8 dsp white sugar
½ pint cider or other white vinegar
2 dsp pickling spice
1 cinnamon stick

Cut the peaches into segments without skinning them – 6 to 8 per peach. If you like the pieces to be bigger, say halves, or quarters, then prick each piece with a sharp fork a couple of times: this allows the pickle to penetrate.

Put all the other ingredients into a pan and bring slowly to the boil. Then simmer for 10 minutes. You may remove the spices now or leave them in. I prefer the latter. Add the peach segments and once they come to the boil, time them carefully. If you want to eat them within a week, simmer for 8 minutes, or until they just start to soften. Let them cool, bottle, and store them in a cool, dark place. Keep in the refrigerator once opened. If you want to save them a couple of months, simmer for only 2–3 minutes depending on size. The reason for the shorter cooking time is that this will keep them firmer and more presentable. Bottle and store as above.

Muesli

The original recipe developed in Switzerland uses the following proportions per helping:

2 tbsp oats
1–2 tsp hazlenuts, chopped
1 small apple, shredded
Honey or unrefined sugar (as little as possible)
Lemon juice to taste
2 tbsp yoghurt
Milk to taste

Frankly, though, you can include what you like. My recommendations are to make a mixture in the proportions of:

6 oz oat flakes
6 oz other mixed grains (I use 2 oz wheat flakes, 2 oz rye flakes, 1 oz millet flakes, 1 oz barley flakes – but you could just use one or two of these).

To that you should add some nuts (hazelnuts are probably the nicest but are even better if toasted before you add them). Seeds are a popular addition; the cheapest and most interesting are shelled pumpkin or sunflower seeds.

Dried fruits add the needed sweetness and I use them instead of adding sugar of any kind. Seedless raisins (especially the black Afghan type) or sliced dried apricots are my favourites. If you really need sugar, sprinkle in some muscovado or demerara sugar, or some golden granulated sugar which flows like white sugar but has the minerals of the softer ones.

Serve the muesli moistened with a little milk and top with yoghurt – but only with plain yoghurt. Fruit yoghurts are very high in calories. A far better idea is to moisten your muesli with a chilled fruit juice, which also makes the addition of fresh fruit more delicious, especially sliced bananas or strawberries.

Breakfast Time Seville Marmalade

Approximately 10-lb yield

The middle of January will for ever be marked on my mental calendar as the time we all began Europe's first breakfast television programme. In fact, it has always been important for any cook because for just a few weeks then we can get the sharp Seville oranges that make the world's best marmalade. There are dozens of recipes, many of them requiring days of soaking and mucking around. This one couldn't be simpler and gives a clear authentic flavour. If you have a pressure cooker it can be done in a tiny fraction of the normal time.

3 lb firm Seville oranges
2 lemons
6 pints water
6 lb sugar, preserving or golden granulated

Wash and halve the fruit. Scoop the seeds out of the oranges and lemons, reserving every drop of juice as you do. Then squeeze any remaining juice from the oranges and lemons and save that. Put the pips into a square of muslin and tie firmly.

Slice the oranges and their remaining flesh as thickly or as thinly as you prefer. The easiest way to get straight strips is to cut the halves in half again, which gives two long, pointed ovals. Cut these across the middle, put on top of each other, cut side above cut side, then slice across the flat edge, working back towards the pointed ends.

Put the cut skins, the halved lemons, and the muslin bag into a large heavy-based saucepan with the water and boil gently until the skins are tender and the water level has reduced by half. Remove the lemons and the bag of pips, squeezing it well.

Heat the sugar thoroughly in a low oven, then add to the mixture. Stir constantly until you are certain it has dissolved, then boil rapidly until the mixture reaches setting point – 220°F (104°C) if you have a jam-making thermometer, or until the surface wrinkles when a drop is allowed to set on a cold plate.

Cool for at least 15 minutes before bottling in warm, clean and dry jars.

Pressure cooker version
The pressure cooker makes marmalade making a pleasure rather than a chore. To adapt the above recipe, cook the fruit as above with only 1 pint of water in your pressure cooker on high pressure for 10 minutes, then release the pressure *slowly.* Remove the lemon and pips and transfer to a bigger pan. Add two pints of water and bring to the boil before adding the 6 lb of preheated sugar.

Pressure Cooker Pink Grapefruit Marmalade

Approximately 3-lb yield

1 or 1½ pink grapefruit	1 pint water
1 lemon	2 lb preserving sugar

The total weight of the grapefruit should be just over 1–1¼ lb maximum. Cut in half and scoop out any seeds you discover. Squeeze the juice into a bowl and save this also. Cut the skin and remaining flesh into strips as thick or as narrow as you like.

Put the juice and strips into a pressure cooker. Add the juice only of the lemon, then mix the lemon pips with any from the grapefruit. Tie up all the pips securely in some muslin and add to the pan. Pour in the water. Cook according to manufacturer's instructions on high pressure for 10 minutes, then release the steam *slowly.* With thin strips, you can probably cook it for just eight minutes.

When you can open the cooker, remove the bag of pips and check that the skins are soft enough to crush between the fingertips.

Now heat the sugar well in a low oven. Reheat the cooked grapefruit in the cooker until boiling, then stir in the sugar. Keep stirring until the sugar is dissolved, then boil rapidly until setting stage is reached – 220°F (104°C), or when the surface wrinkles when a small drop is allowed to set on a cold plate.

Remove from heat and let rest for at least 10 minutes, stirring once or twice before bottling in warm, clean and dry bottles. If you do not wait that short time the peel will possibly float once the marmalade is bottled.

Note: Do not be alarmed if your pink grapefruit has few or no seeds. The thick skin and the inclusion of all the pulp will still ensure an excellent set.

If you do not have a pressure cooker, cook the skins and pips in 2 pints of water until really soft, then proceed as above. It may take a couple of hours for the softening to occur.

Christmas Time

A Sensible Christmas Turkey

I don't understand people who groan about the trouble they are expected to take over the turkey for Christmas Day. When you get down to it, they are usually complaining about two things – first the time they have to get up to cook the damned thing, and second the horror of thinking up ways to use the leftovers. Both these are simply solved. One – you buy a smaller turkey. And two – almost all the commercial recommendations I've ever seen for cooking turkeys are ludicrously overestimated, simply to avoid the risk of salmonella through undercooking frozen turkeys, or to ensure that wodges of stuffing inside the bird are cooked through.

Take a deep breath, think the whole thing through again, think small and think simple. Do those, and follow my *Breakfast Time* Turkey Guide, and you'll enjoy both Christmas Day and the turkey. You might even look forward to the leftovers. A Christmas blessing indeed!

Here are the basic rules for the sensible cooking of turkeys.

1 Never stuff the body cavity. This increases the cooking time so much that you overcook the bird to cook the stuffing. As well, most stuffings will draw juices from the breast meat, quite the reverse of what you need.

2 Loosely fill the body cavity with things that will *create* moisture – sliced apples and onions, chopped oranges and lemons, that sort of thing.

3 Never truss a bird. Trussing is a legacy from the days of spits, when legs all over the place meant the spit would not turn evenly. By trussing legs close to the body you vastly increase the time needed to cook the thighs and thus overcook the breast. With the legs left free they will cook as fast as the breast.

4 Never, ever, cook the turkey on its back, except perhaps for the very last few minutes. Whilst on its back, the juices from the breast meat run out into the cavity where they are of little use. Instead you should cook a bird on its sides so the juices run from side to side. Makes sense, doesn't it?

5 Always turn a turkey on to its breast or leave it on its side when it comes from the oven. This too is to ensure the juices run back into the breast and stay there. Remember always to leave a cooked bird at least 20–30 minutes before carving, so that the juice stays in the flesh. It will stay really hot for much longer than this.

6 Remove the wish-bone before cooking – you'll see why in a minute.

7 And before doing any of this, take absolute care to ensure a frozen bird is thoroughly defrosted. Best bet, both for flavour and for safety from salmonella poisoning, is to order a fresh one.

Basic Recipe

8–12-lb oven-ready turkey
3 lb approximately stuffing mixture
Bacon or muslin soaked in butter

A turkey this size will easily feed 8 or more people and still leave a lot over.

Stretch the skin around the neck and then, with a sharp-pointed knife, carefully cut out the wish-bone. Stuff the turkey's neck end or, even better, between the breast skin and the flesh. To do this, you simply slide your hand or fingers between the flesh and skin and gently move forwards, from the breast end, lifting and stretching the skin. Work sideways, too, lifting the skin between the body and the legs, and over the legs. Stuffing can then be inserted, and once that is done, you should pat and smooth the bird back into a natural, but plumper, shape. The great advantage of stuffing in this way is that the bird will constantly be basted with the fats and the juices of the ingredients and, being protected from direct heat, the flesh will be infinitely moister. Put something that will create steam inside the bird – onions and oranges are my favourites.

Place the bird, untrussed remember, on its side in a roasting tray, then put it directly into a preheated oven Gas Mark 7/425°F/220°C for 10 minutes. Turn the bird on its other side and cook for the same amount of time.

Now drape the side of the bird with bacon, or with muslin that has been generously soaked in butter – you will need 6–8 oz at least. Reduce the heat of the oven to Gas Mark 4/350°F/180°C and cook the bird for 12–15 minutes per lb (allowing for the weight of the stuffing), turning from side to side every half-hour. (For ease and safety while turning the cooking bird, simply use clean oven gloves, which will become impregnated with fat and juice and need to be washed. But better dirty gloves than disappointingly dry turkey.) A small bird needs to be cooked for the lesser amount of time per pound.

Test by inserting a skewer or fork into the upper thigh. If the juices run clear without a suspicion of pink, the breast will also be beautifully cooked – but never pierce the breast or it will drain of moisture.

Rest the bird in a warmish place for at least 20 minutes, still turning from side to side. If it is not a very big bird you could simply tip it forward onto its breast, but support the weight a little with foil or uncooked potatoes or you will squash the meat.

Now comes the moment when the reason for removing the wish-bone is made clear. Instead of letting the turkey grow cold, and your guests grow restless while you struggle with the carving, you are able to take a long sharp knife and, starting on the long breast bone, slice an entire side of the breast right off, following the curve of the rib cage. Put the whole breast onto a carving dish and you can cut it into even slices in a minute. Good idea that, isn't it?

Now, here are two stuffings and some sauces to go with the turkey. The second stuffing, based on dried apricots and mint, is so good that people stopped me in the street to tell me that it had made their best Christmas ever.

Chestnut Stuffing

For an 8-lb turkey

1½–2 lb coarse pork sausages (bratwurst or Toulouse are best, otherwise buy the meatiest you can find)
½ lb fine sausage meat
1-lb tin unsweetened chestnut purée
½–1 lb whole cooked chestnuts or up to 8 oz dehydrated chestnuts
1 strip orange peel (3″ × ½″) and red wine (see recipe)
1 large orange
2 or 3 tbsp finely chopped celery leaf
Coarse black pepper
At least 2 tsp cinnamon
1 tsp ground nutmeg
½ tsp ground mace
½ tsp ground cloves
Port or brandy to taste
Dried breadcrumbs if necessary

Take the filling out of the sausages and add to the sausage meat. Mix in the chestnut purée, then coarsely chop the chestnuts; the most flavoursome of all are the Italian dehydrated chestnuts, available only at Christmas time. Cover these with liquid, perhaps half red wine, half water; simmer them with a strip of orange peel until plump and soft.

Grate in the rind of one large orange (you may as well squeeze in the juice too). Add the celery leaf, lots of pepper and, most important, several generous teaspoons of cinnamon, the ground nutmeg, mace and cloves. Mix together with a generous helping of port or brandy (or both), trying not to break up the whole chestnuts too much. Break off a small amount and fry in a pan to test the flavour and texture: if it is too wet, add some good-quality dried breadcrumbs (not golden) and test again. One year I also added whole cranberries which were a great success.

This mixture can be made in advance and frozen and, if made quite firmly, is a real sensation when stuffed under the breast skin. Provided you allow the bird to rest for a good 20 or even 30 minutes before carving, the stuffing will be firm enough to cut into slices.

Only use as much under the skin as looks sensible; cook the rest as individual patties in the tin or stuffed into the neck end.

Apricot and Mint Stuffing

2 lb coarse pork sausages (bratwurst or Toulouse are best, otherwise buy the meatiest you can find)
½ lb fine sausage meat
½ lb dried apricots
Grated rind and juice of a large orange
1 dsp dried mint
Coarse black pepper
At least 2 tsp ground cinnamon
1 tsp ground nutmeg
½ tsp ground mace
½ tsp ground cloves

Remove the pork sausages from their skins, and mix thoroughly with the sausage meat. Slice the apricots into strips, and add to the sausage mixture. Add the rest of the ingredients and mix thoroughly.

Cranberry Sauces

Two sauces for turkey, goose or game that allow you to add your own touches. A small pot of both or either is a welcome Christmas present.

Cooked Cranberry Sauce

1 lb fresh or defrosted cranberries
¼ pint good red or white wine or port (Cyprus Ruby would do)
1 cinnamon stick
6–8 oz white or brown sugar
1–2 dsp blanched matchsticks of orange peel

Put the cranberries in a saucepan with the wine or port and the cinnamon stick. Bring slowly to the boil and simmer until the skins start to pop. Remove from the heat at once, then stir in the sugar and orange peel. Remove the cinnamon stick. Do *not* add the sugar while the berries are heating or the skins will toughen. This can be served hot or cold.

Uncooked Cranberry Relish

This recipe, which I brought back from New England, is virtually unknown here. It is uncooked and improves if made in advance and matured, just as with mincemeat.

1 lb cranberries
1 small cooking apple (peeled and cored)
1 whole orange
½ lemon (including peel)
½ lb sugar
Brandy, rum or port to taste

Chop up the lemon and orange roughly, removing any pips but leaving the skin. Then chop or mince finely, together with the cranberries and the apple. A food processor is the simplest way if you have one. Add sugar to taste and leave at least 24 hours. Flavour further with a little brandy, rum or port. This will last ages if kept in a refrigerator.

Spiced Salt Beef

Serves 6–8 or more, depending on the sharpness of your knife

Spiced beef was a great Victorian favourite but takes ages to make from fresh. This one starts with readily available salt beef. Serve it hot on Christmas Day or Boxing Day or keep it cold to cut into when you are feeling exhausted.

- 4–5 lb lean salt beef – silverside is better than brisket
- 3 oz brown sugar
- 2 tsp black peppercorns
- 1 tsp ground mace
- 1 tsp ground nutmeg
- 1 tsp dry mustard powder
- 1 tsp ground coriander
- ½ tsp ground cloves – at least
- 6 large dry bay leaves
- 4–6 oz brown sugar
- ¼–½ pint port wine
- 3–6 cloves garlic (optional)
- 1–1½ lb mixed root vegetables and onion (optional)
- 10–12 crushed juniper berries (optional)

Pound the sugar and peppercorns together, mix in the spices. Crumble the bay leaves finely and mix those in also. Crush and chop the garlic if you are using it. Stir in evenly.

Stand the beef on a substantial dish or in a bowl and press the spice mixture firmly and evenly into the surface. Then wrap the whole bowl (not just the meat) in several layers of aluminium foil and leave in the refrigerator for 4 to 5 days, turning from time to time.

Put the meat and all the spices into a large saucepan and cover with cold water. Add most of the second quantity of sugar plus the port, which can be cheap Cyprus Ruby. Add the vegetables, if used, for extra flavour as well as the crushed juniper berries. Bring slowly to the boil and simmer gently for about 4 hours but do not boil it ragged. Add extra sugar during cooking to balance the flavour if it seems overspiced.

The vegetables will be useless, but the stock may be freshened with lots of parsley and served as a sauce for the hot version. To serve it cold, let it cool in the cooking liquid, which gives more moistness and tenderness.

Cranberry Molasses Pudding

Serves 4–6

Another standard of my Christmas season since I discovered it in America years ago. Spiced and topped with a festive crown of red berries, it makes a fabulous light alternative for those who dislike the heavy traditional pudding.

½ lb cranberries, fresh or frozen	½ lb self-raising flour
3 oz butter	¼ pint molasses, warm
4 dsp demerara sugar	⅛ pint milk, warm
2 tsp mixed spice	1 tsp vanilla or maple essence

Using some of the butter, grease a 3-pint pudding basin and put 2 oz of the cranberries, half the sugar, and 1 tsp of the mixed spice on the base. Roughly chop the rest of the cranberries, but leave many of them cut no smaller than halves. Do not chop finely.

Mix 4 oz of the chopped cranberries into the flour – you will have a quarter of the original amount of cranberries still unused. Warm your can of molasses by standing it in hot water, then measure out the ¼ pint. Add to it the milk, remaining butter and vanilla or maple essence.

Mix the molasses-flavoured liquid into the flour and turn the mixture into the prepared pudding basin. Cover with the remaining cranberries, sugar and mixed spice.

Cover the basin with several layers of cloth or foil, remembering to fold a pleat in the top to allow for expansion. Steam on a trivet in a covered saucepan for 2 hours. Tip out of the basin and serve with Old-Fashioned Butter Sauce or Orange Zabaglione Sauce.

Old-Fashioned Butter Sauce

¼ lb butter	¼ pint single or double cream
¼ lb sugar	2 tsp vanilla or maple essence

Mix together all the ingredients. Simmer for 5 minutes. Rum could be used instead of the essence. Serve hot.

Orange Zabaglione Sauce for Christmas Pudding

Serves 4–6

Rum and brandy butter do not belong with Christmas puddings but with mince pies. Served with a thin rum-flavoured custard or this foamy orange sauce your pudding will be much more balanced and enjoyable – and more authentic, too.

- 3 large egg yolks, *or* 2 medium or small whole eggs
- 1 oz caster sugar
- ¼ pint mixed orange juice and white wine
- Grated rind of half an orange

Beat the egg yolks or eggs together with the sugar until light and creamy coloured. While you are doing that, have a saucepan of water boiling into which your bowl will fit: a copper bowl gives the best results by far.

Once the sugar is well dissolved in the beaten eggs, add the juice, wine and grated rind and put the bowl over the boiling water. A hand-operated egg beater is best for the next operation unless you are experienced with a hand whisk and have lots of muscles. Keep beating quite fast until the foam just starts to thicken – you can tell simply by lifting the beater from the mixture from time to time. When it drops back in globs rather than dribbles, it is ready.

Take the bowl from the heat and keep whisking furiously until it has stopped setting. Serve it immediately on your Christmas pudding or Cranberry Molasses pudding, or make it in advance and serve it cold.

Bought Mincemeat Improved

This marvellous trick beats the problem of oversweet commercial mincemeats. But it won't work unless you use the dark, sharp marmalade specified.

- 1-lb jar mincemeat
- 2 generous tbsp vintage or thick-cut marmalade
- 3 tbsp brandy or dark rum
- 1 tsp cinnamon

Mix all the ingredients together and use as you would ordinary mincemeat.

St Clement Danes' Mincemeat

For approximately 8 lb

I discovered, during my researches into the best mincemeat recipe for *Breakfast Time* viewers, that many old ones used purées of cooked whole lemons. So I followed that technique but added oranges too, hence the name. The sharpness and flavour they give will convert you to this forever, and it makes excellent inexpensive Christmas gifts.

2 oranges
2 lemons, medium
1½–2 lb large Bramley apples
1 lb Barbados or muscovado sugar
1 lb stoned raisins
1 lb currants
1 lb beef suet
4 oz chopped peel
¼–½ pint brandy, black rum, orange liqueur, or a mixture (optional)
1 dsp ground mace (optional)
1 dsp ground cloves (optional)
1 dsp ground allspice (optional)

Strain the juice from the oranges and lemons and put all the rest of the citrus fruit (skin and pulp) to cook until soft enough to purée. (This takes about 5 minutes if you have a pressure cooker – use ½ pint water.)

Peel and chop the apples finely and add to the juice. Then add the sugar, raisins, currants, beef suet and chopped peel. This is excellent as it is, with neither alcohol nor spices, but you can add either or both according to your budget or preferences.

Put into very clean containers with as little extra air as possible. Seal and leave in a cool place for at least two weeks.

Options: A good use for mincemeat is to line the base of an apple pie with it. Sprinkle the apple with a little grated orange peel and spice, too, if you like.